EVERY
DAY
WE GET
MORE
ILLEGAL

EVERY
DAY
WE GET
MORE
ILLEGAL

Juan Felipe Herrera

CITY LIGHTS BOOKS | San Francisco

Cover art: "Detention X" Prismacolor markers on found cardboard,
  by Juan Felipe Herrera, 2019
Cover design by em dash

Library of Congress Cataloging-in-Publication Data
Names: Herrera, Juan Felipe, author.
Title: Every day we get more illegal / Juan Felipe Herrera.
Description: San Francisco : City Lights Books, 2020.
Identifiers: LCCN 2019056674 | ISBN 9780872868281 (trade paperback)
Subjects: LCGFT: Poetry.
Classification: LCC PS3558.E74 E88 2020 | DDC 811/.54--dc23
LC record available at https://lccn.loc.gov/2019056674

Abundant thank you's to the following online and offline publishers for taking my work
to many readers:

Boston Review, Academy of American Poets, Poetry Foundation, *Love's Executive Order,
Best American Poetry 2020, Pushcart Prize Anthology 2019, Resistance, Rebellion, Life:
50 Poems Now, Poems for Political Disaster, Tales of Two Americas: Stories of Inequality in
a Divided Nation*

NOTE:
"todavía estoy aquí the deported father said" was written in conversation with the
photography portfolio of Jonathan Maldonado, grade 12, Essex Street Academy, New York,
NY. Presented in the 2017 National Catalog of the Scholastic Art and Writing Awards.

City Lights Books are published at the City Lights Bookstore
261 Columbus Avenue, San Francisco, California, 94133
www.citylights.com

for all the migrants, immigrants and refugees suffering from the border installations within the United States, at the border crossing and throughout Latin America. for a borderless society and world, made of relentless unity and kindness and giving.

for Margarita de Las Flores, the seer, love.

for Mama Lucha and Papa Felipe, pioneers, givers of life. for my children, grandchildren and great-grandchildren. for all my familias in California, Oregon, New Mexico, Arizona, and New York. for my agent, Kendra Marcus, and my editor and publisher, Elaine Katzenberger at City Lights, San Francisco. Countless gracias.

for all my friends, bards and artists, teachers and professors, editors and publishers, for the many gifts you offered.

for my dear companions at the Library of Congress, the Poetry and Literature Center, and all who greeted me and guided me while I was Poet Laureate of the United States. Warm-hearted appreciations for Dr. James Billington, Head Librarian of Congress, for inviting me to be the Laureate, and for director, Rob Casper and the Poetry staff for their friendship and for mapping the journey.

And once again, many bows to all the beautiful students and schools that opened their doors and hearts.

This boundless desire of being
— *Francisco X.Alarcón, "Never Alone," Snake Poems*

Oh, ring, ring, open wide and let us out!
— *Anne Frank, "Monday Evening, November 8, 1943," Diary of Anne Frank*

contents

ADDRESS BOOK FOR THE FIREFLY

ON THE ROAD NORTH #1 1

America We Talk About It 3

Open 4

Basho & Mandela 5

You Just Don't Talk About It 6

Listen to Elias Canetti 8

Don't Push the Button 9

ADDRESS BOOK FOR THE FIREFLY

ON THE ROAD NORTH #2 11

[interruption] 13

[1] 14

[2] 15

[3] 16

[4] 17

[5] 18

Ko Un Says 19

Touch the Earth (once again) 20

Roll Under the Waves 21

Fuimos visibles / We Were the Visible Ones 22

Enuf 24

**ADDRESS BOOK FOR THE FIREFLY
ON THE ROAD NORTH #3** 27

Interview w/a Border Machine 29
Color Tense 33
i am not a paid protestor 35

**ADDRESS BOOK FOR THE FIREFLY
ON THE ROAD NORTH #4** 43

& no one knew them 45
Everyday we get more illegal 46
todavía estoy aquí the deported father said 48
border fever 105.7 degrees 50

**ADDRESS BOOK FOR THE FIREFLY
ON THE ROAD NORTH #5** 51

i want to speak of unity 53
Ten Thousand Lives 54

**ADDRESS BOOK FOR THE FIREFLY
ON THE ROAD NORTH #6** 55

come with me 57

Every Day We Get More Illegal

Address Book for the Firefly

on the Road North #1

Your consciousness
is ever expanding
onto infinity

America We Talk About It

Summer Journals — August 8 2017

— every day of the week. It is not easy. First I had to learn. Over decades — to take care of myself. Are you listening. I had to learn. I had to gain, pebble by pebble, seashell by seashell, the courage to listen to my self. My true inner self. For that I had to push you aside. It was not easy I had pushed aside my mother my father my self in that artificial stairway of becoming you to be inside of you — after years I realized perhaps too late there was no way I could bring them back I could not rewind the clock. But I did — I could do one thing. I could care. Now we — are here.

Open

as the leaf as the sidewalk as the tear & the iris as the casket
upon visitation as the door when the twig school opens
as the tongue that knows no rule as the trees unto
vastness as the seed on its first day as the root twisting
as the face when freedom strikes lightning freedom as the crystal
upon sudden awareness as the waterfall rushing toward more
openness as the walk of everything that walks
as the shame lock when it breaks out of your skin

Basho & Mandela

As Basho has said —
it is a narrow road to the Deep North — as Mandela has said
the haphazard segregation later became a well-orchestrated
    segregation
— as Basho has said the journey began with an attained
    awareness
that at any moment you can become a weather-exposed skeleton
— think of us in this manner
these are notes for your nourishment — hold them
as bowls of kindness
from journeys of bravery
the will to seek & find the sudden turning rivers & the dawn-eyed

      freedom

You Just Don't Talk About It

Lissen: you just don't

talk about it the rape the endless scrubbing washing self
lacerations the never ending self-whipping the deep down
smoldering stone trauma growing up crooked tree growing up
silence ocean storm growing tsunami without a sky ceiling you
prefer the holiday merchandise the rational vacuum you just
don't care about the pushed out the stopped out the forced out
the starved out the fenced out the shot down the cut back the
asphalted out on the other side of the track the suicided the
hanged w/ a bedsheet of nothing in the cell of nothing with
no one at the gate the segregated tier the jailed forever the
imprisoned forever the denied the woman ambling alone 79
yrs old going nowhere to Social Services you don't talk about
fires inside inside us inside the young with no-lunches and the
no-books and the no-schools and the no-parents just needles and
drunkdrunk streets drunk walls drunk hotels drunk bathroom
tiles drunk you don't care about the trans teens the taste of acid
the taste of plutonium about the nugget of larva of decay in
our milk and juice and you don't care about the pesticide skin
of uncle Timoteo hauling Mendota cotton and melons on the
hammer lane of the 99 and the Spanish Arabic Chinese Hmong
Filipino spoken in the yard yes you want one language one
religion one dollar for all except the moguls the mogul oil the
mogul pipelines in pajamas I know you heard this all before you

6

have the smart language your lawyers lawyers for your lawyers
you have your corporate privacy but you do not notice you do
not walk you do not enter you do not get near you stay there
where you are at this moment you do not care about the cold-
shot murder in the car at the tip of your open mouth gun you
do not care about the addictions you unleashed you do not care
about the lands you stole from under our feet you do not care
about smearing our faces across the screen and never say a word
when you hit the holy bank you do not care in your pyramid
of insulations you do not care about those who fight for you
write for you live for you act for you study for you dance for you
parade for you paint and construct for you carry you build you
inform you feed you nanny you clean you vacuum for you swipe
the grease off your clothes chef for you serve you teach you carry
carry you rock you to sleep and console you the rape the assault
the segregation the jailing the deportations upon deportations
the starving the ones curled up on the freezing detention corners
because they wanted to touch you to meet you against all odds
and you — you
        just don't talk about it

Listen to Elias Canetti

Are you a crowd
— are you a hunting pack — are you a domestication plasma,
half machine-half skin production, are you a punishment-love
hypnosis, are you a Segmenter without eyes or heart or blood,
are you the remoteness that is all we know now, are you the
barcode of humans at so many gates, checking-in, interrogated,
zapped by desolation at every turn, are you the Symbol-maker of
detachment, are you the finger exercises taught to monkeys, are
you the follower of *"the killers are always the powerful,"* are you
the Force-eater

somewhere in there
there is change — Change-speakers
Change-churners even   in the tiniest things

    — a falling leaf

Don't Push the Button

Just don't understand why so many want you to push the button
don't push it please don't push it
you are making me nervous I am slouching toward nowhere
art is not enough
performance is not enough
something is missing don't push it to fill the vacuum
it is something that has not been solved before it is that simple
you must find that achieve that it is not too late
the button of course is not the answer of course
it provides an ounce or two of arousal
similar to the walls of Patrols
similar to the 30 billion dollar aircraft carrier you just set out
into the metal oceans
do not push it I am nervous something is off-kilter
it is beyond words beyond poetry beyond Milton and Sappho
it is beyond Paz and Ko Un it is beyond all the African
drummers it is closer to the ashes of South Sudan and
the green skulls of a Mexican State I cannot mention and
the massacres the massacres so many massacres in plain sight
do not push it
we will fall leaves or snow it is that simple
we will not have to wait
for 3 billion more years to perish
as the solar orb dissolves and cuts the forces that hold us

do not push do not listen to the war provosts beside you
come here where we sit
in this annex between walls of a nondescript house
where we shudder
where we write and string the guitar the fervent bones we
spin on the floor do not push it

Address Book for the Firefly
on the Road North #2

we are merely
seekers wanderers
moving alongside
the mountains

[interruption]

[1]

underneath the wall there is a crust of war operations it extends
    far beyond the lines it opens its fibers & cables across global
    nets yes
& there are weaponized hormigas carrying out the orders
    underneath——the wall

it is more than an arbitrary stop or as it is called the border it is
an arrangement of agreements of always-war why is that when all
we desire is peace bread water clothes work a thatched roof — &
humanity — most of all

[2]

we notice the interconnections of war operators
when we happen to

peer under the message of the wall into the apparatus it is true

[3]

underneath the code of the wall things are always
in motion

    while we wait to cross

[4]

yet we continue on with the new exemplar of what life is the one
we carry as we pass as our ancestors have for more than 170 years
  above us the watchtowers below the crust of war operations
  inside

[5]

above us & in our hands & on our forehead there is a light
we call it star a star a starstar a star a starstar

      a star

Ko Un Says

                                        Leap
every human being in the village is an ever-opening story
yes you must write about each one — it is the bravest gesture
                                        you must
let your hands find the water
drag out from the village well
everyone stands with their palms to their face they wait for you
now

there is a line of quail leading to the meadows
outside the city the persimmons are exactly
the color they should be

Touch the Earth (once again)

This is what we do:

this is what the cotton truck driver does:
this is what the tobacco leaf roller does:
this is what the washer-woman & the laundry worker does:
this is what the grape & artichoke worker does:
not to mention the cucumber workers —
not to mention the spinach & beet workers
not to mention the poultry woman workers
not to mention the packing house workers &
the winery workers & the lettuce & broccoli
& peach & apricot & squash & apple &
that almost-magical watermelon
& the speckled melon & the honey-dew the workers
this is what they do:

notice: how they bend in the fires no one sees
notice: their ecstatic colors & their knotted shirts
notice: where they cash
their tiny & wrinkled checks & pay stubs:
stand in that small-town desert sundries store
then walk out they do & stall for a moment they do
underneath this colossal tree with its condor-wings
shedding solace for a second or two notice:
how they touch the earth — for you

Roll Under the Waves

we roll under the waves
not above them we body surf and somehow we lose
the momentum there are memories trailing us empty orange
and hot pink bottles of medicines left behind
buried next to a saguaro there are baby backpacks
and a thousand shoes and a thousand gone steps
leading in the four directions without destinations
there are men lying face down forever and women
dragging under the fences and children still running with
torn faces all the way to Tucson leathery and peeling
there are vigilantes with skull dust on their palms
and the trigger and the sputum and the moon with
its pocked hope and its blessings and its rotations into the spikes
there is a road forgotten with a tiny sweet roof of twigs
and a black griddle threaded with songs like the one
about el contrabando from El Paso there is nothing
a stolen land forgotten too a stolen life branded and
tied and thrown into the tin patrol box with flashes of trees
and knife-shaped rivers and the face of my mother Luz and
water running next to the animals still thrashing choking
their low burnt violin muffled screams in rings
of roses across the mountains

Fuimos visibles

fuimos visibles luego invisibles fuimos visibles
mar y geometría ocelotl y pantera luego invisibles luego más
invisibles luego pirámide luego azufre luego selva audaz
luego hilo de orígenes luego cereal de esclavo luego visibles
luego manifestación a través estancias y bulevares luego
invisibles luego oficinas de paja en los fuegos
luego visibles piedra de tiempo luz y más luz girando
luego invisibles sumas divisiones luego visibles por un
momento existimos jaguares brisas entre los cementos entre
los camiones y eslabones entre los senderos migrantes

We Were the Visible Ones

we were visible then invisible we were visible
ocean & geometry ocelotl & panther then invisible then deeper
invisible then pyramid then sulfur then rainforest audacious
origin of strings then the field grain of slaves then visible
then lines of protest across tiny ranches & boulevards then
invisible ones then offices of straw in the fires
then visible time-stone light & more light twirlers
then the invisible ones more sums & divisions then visible for a
moment we existed jaguars sea mist in between the cement in
between lorries & shackles in between migrant torches

Enuf

used to think I was not American enuf
used to think I would never be American enuf
i never thought of it
was in it & out   again

used to think How could I ever dress that way
did you ever meet Sadie Hawkins or Tennessee Ernie Ford
used to think Where am I Who am I — a bit too much
used to live on the outside of where you lived
used to throw stones at your window on the way to catechism
used to think I was always on borrowed time
used to knock on your door every day but no one answered
on Halloween I walked with thousands with an empty bag
& when I rolled back to apartment #2 at 2044 Mission Street
I delighted
in my hobo torn-pants get-up with my Shinola sideburns
my motion was always angled in the opposite direction
was a green-yellow-brown Mexican in a Greyhound bus
you ever noticed green-yellow-brown Mexicans at the depot
was every color & tone & texture except White or Brown
was Indian somewhere in Central Mexico on the outside
of Tepito the deepest barrio in Mexico City where
no one asked questions
was an expert at signing my mother's Alien Registration Card
was an unlicensed professional window shopper

— can you identify the contours and chromatics of a Bulova
a Hamilton a Wittenhauer an Elgin a Longines
my hobbies included watching people go places
lose myself on Indio Street in San Diego
used to think suits were impossible — still do
clip-ties were doable used clothes most appropriate
i found ecstasy in listening to mountain wolves
outside our trailer on the outskirts of the other side of the tracks
on the other mesa of the road few passed
the wolves sounded as if water was near or
as if they were spiraling out from the moon
used to think I was not American enuf
not even in the welfare offices where I employed
superb translation skills for my mother
was a city wonderer a believer in magic a kid who
pierced his left eye throwing scissors at nothing
noticed a colt being born tearing through the life-curtain
my mother wrote notes about my daily progress
into a tiny address book the color of lipstick
the size of three postage stamps
this is not a poor-boy story
this is a pioneer story
this is your story
America are you listening
my father walked to the ocean waters with a jar
in his hand bowed down & filled it & said
"This will heal you"

i did not know how to melt how to fall into another body
spoke a language you could not hear
listened to stories you never told
sang songs you did not sing
had my own way of tracking the sun
used to think I was not American enuf
was filled with dreamy maps of my grandmother Juanita ambling
to Júarez during the Mexican Revolution & my uncles Roberto
Chente & Jeno lacing up their Army leggings at Fort Bliss in 1919
my mother twangin' a guitar without a stage or land to sing

used to think I was not American enuf
now it is the other way around

Address Book for the Firefly

on the Road North #3

when we reach
the family shrine
made of twigs bitten cloth
shrubs & dirt

we bow

Interview
w/a Border Machine

can you please state your name
        Xochitl Tzompantli
what kind of name is that
                it was given to me by an indian woman
                        black hair long black shawl — it
                        means *Skull Rack Flower*
well let's get to business here   why
are you here in the first place
                i do not
                talk about
                that   all i know
                                                eyes
                swim before
                me   a river
                eyes
                fall upon   me w/candle
                  fire in their blood
                to   come —
what do you tell them
                nothing
why are you speaking to me
        — dying falling   wars

everything inside of   me is
alive & dying at the
sametime against each   other
what do you know about war you are nothing
but a wall

a lie touch me
like they
touch me
climb upon me
like they give
their deepest bones — i
carry a severed withering
night unto night

inside
you will find   your name
written on a piece of flesh
you are a bit dramatic i am just interested in
a simple & short interview
of course everyone is
why are you here besides being a hard-working
border apparatus

i give you
meaning

come on that is easy
every one
eats from my flesh

                                        calls me from afar
                        nails me   pour themselves
                        into me   take me to the   sky threads
                        i feed
                        meaning i
                        prepare a place   more for you
                        than for   the ones here
what you are saying
                            it does
                                    not matter
well ok ok what about your friends plans projects
        hobbies like that
                    i do not have such
                            things as   friends
ok well we are done
                wait —
                        my name is Xochitl Tzompantli
                        Skull Rack Flower i am
                                    the life-cutter the eater
                    watchtowers guards artillery
                            wires & codes & dogs &
                            filth nourish me
                                                i provide
            ghosts unclaimed that tie you to a circle
                    of tortured faces that on occasion
        appears as a flower on your suit

                                31

i
        bow down to them i remember them
                i ask them to
                        forgive me but
all they see is

                you

Color Tense
(a fracture of power and paradigm)

i had a color > there is no color > i was bronze > we do not have
bronze > i was golden sienna ochre > there are no siennas or golden
siennas or ochres here > we had colors > we have no colors > we
had faces with colors > there are no faces with colors > we stood up
we danced all the colors > there is no standing the color dances are
illegal haven't you heard > we had colors on our hands and scarves >

              i told you
              no colors
              no colors
              no color shoes
              or faces or noses
              no illegal scarves >

we held up an ancient disk with the lost inscriptions
& stories of our colors our bronze >

                        we are burning
                        that vessel those signs
                        those words those long
                        lines there are
                        no colors now >

we dreamed our colors > it is not useful to dream >
we dreamed about our colors > it is not useful
                        there are no colors now >

we brought in a new time > this is the new time >
we wanted our mothers to bend their ears to the
lost stories the burned stories the fettered
stories the ones that rose up from the ancient
disk > this is the new time this eye is the new
eye this voice is the new voice this chair with
the wingspan upright is the new chair > the disc
was soaked in blood > it is a new time > it was what
we called for > you have the wrong time > it was our
song > your blood is wrong it is too small it
is filled with holes your songs are illegal no colors
they are not useful your time is filled with holes
your blood is too small > i am walking away >
that is permissible > i am leaving you here > that
is practical > i do not want the disk > what
did you say what > the color is
everywhere >

i do not see it >
golden sienna spins right through you >
where > everywhere > your time is too small >

                    my time is now >
the time is now >>

i am not a paid protestor

you are a paid
protestor

no

we know
you are being
paid

no

we know you
are being
paid
at this
very moment

no

we know
you are
being funded
by shadow
investors

that is
incorrect

                    we know
                    that you meet w/
                    shadow
                    investors interested
                    in overturning
                    our
                    structures

i am not
concerned
with
your
structures as a matter of fact you do not
have any so-called structures at this time

                         that's what you
                         have been
                         instructed
                         to say —
                         we know

no
you do not

                         you have
                         been instructed
                         to launch

a spiral a ring
across the
edifice
to install
a fracture
a severance
a crevice

what are you saying
how do you know

we know
you do things &
then you do
them

i am
protesting
that
is
all

no
you
are   not

i am
here
of my own
free will

there
is no
such
thing

yes
that is why
i am
protesting

you
are paid

listen:
i am
protesting
out
of
my
own
free
      will

there
is
no such
thing

how about
some candy

you are
bribing me

i don't do that

of course

how about some
candy

i don't do
that

i got ginseng

no way
never

take
my frog

you
got
to be
kidding

take it

                        you are
                        out
                        of your
                        mind

it's a meditation frog

                        never in
                        your
                        life

you can
meditate
with it

                        we're
                        getting
                        nowhere

excellent

                        what?

we
are
on the
way

                        i am
                        hitting

the button

get out
of your
bubble

i
am
hitting the
button

what
button

the
deportation
button

wow

you hear
me

wow

i am hitting
it

it's
not
the deportation
button —

push
it

you are
tricking
me

it's
the mass hypnosis button

you
are out
of your
gourd sir

push it

i
don't
want
to
push
it

push
it

Address Book for the Firefly

on the Road North #4

ancestors
passed these trails
their designs

offer kindness to the timeless trees
they recognize you

& no one knew them

& no one knew them

For the ones taken in the rustle of thorns w/o stars
For the ones the color of water who slowly grew peaceful
Face down on the spikes of asphalt
For the ones I longed to give lettuce who turned fast away
When they noticed a truck-man hunched scribbling
Near the fence they could have been
Feathered round & desire-shaped w/
Black rubber-like feet & elegant noses
In search for a way out

This endless container
Lagoon of shadows

Everyday We Get More Illegal

Yet the peach tree
still rises
& falls with fruit & without
birds eat it the sparrows fight
our desert

      burns with trash & drug
it also breathes & sprouts
vines & maguey

laws pass laws with scientific walls
detention cells   husband
          with the son
        the wife &
the daughter who
married a citizen
they stay behind broken   slashed

half-shadows in the apartment to
deal out the day

     & the puzzles
another law then   another
Mexican
     Indian
        spirit exile

migration   sky
the grass is mowed then blown
by a machine   sidewalks are empty
clean & the Red Shouldered Hawk

peers
down — from
an abandoned wooden dome
          an empty field

it is all in between the light
every day this   changes a little

yesterday homeless &
w/o papers   Alberto
left for Denver a Greyhound bus he said
where they don't check you

walking working
under the silver darkness
     walking   working

our mind
our life

todavía estoy aquí the deported father said

still here i
am still here at times
still here in half-light at times with you
peering at this odd-angled orb
todavía estoy aquí for you yes para tí todavía still here i
am for you todavía still here it is true para tí for you in half-
light it is this way still full face toward you   still here for you
at times i sleep at times all i can see barely at times the shadow
that is me not me it is here still the door open at times burns
w/o me even though i am still here todavía for you para tí
on occasion you
                  notice me look down i look down a smile
yes a tiny smile comes to me for you para tí todavía aquí here
for you here i am both of us
in darker light filters than the last time
we stood together todavía still here on this half-orb
both of us a father
in a clean washed shirt after a scalding shower todavía
still you me w/o
the shadow at times the shadow
i cannot tell i sleep the blankets folded and unfolded todavía
still here para tí for you   todavía

todavía estoy aquí para tí still here

                           i am still here here yes for you

                                       i am

border fever 105.7 degrees

— for Jakelin Amei Rosemery, 7 yrs old, from Guatemala, with a fever
of 105.7, who died in custody and for 8 yr old, Felipe Gómez Alonzo, also
from Guatemala, who died under custody of Customs and Border Protection
on 12-24-18. For all migrant and immigrant children, and their families
separated on the road north.

     why do you cry
those are not screams you hear across this cage
it is   a symphony — the border guard says

there is a girl   *up ahead*
made of sparkles   *is she*   *me or*
is   *she*
  dead

                        on the custody floor
                           105.7 degrees

where do I go where did they go
where do I go to breathe no more

        a lost flame a firefly
      dressing for freedom

                  where did   she go

Address Book for the Firefly
on the Road North #5

if you
climb faster
than the others

you will
reach the place
you have dreamed of

                          yet
you will miss something
you will miss the journey of the
whole

i want to speak of unity

         — i want to speak of unity that indescribable thing
we have been speaking of since '67 when I first stepped into LA
with a cardboard box luggage piece I was distracted by you
your dances askew & somersaults the kind you see
at shopping centers
& automobile super sale events — the horns &
bayonets most of all
I wanted to pierce the density the elixirs of everything something
like Max Beckmann did in that restaurant painting of '37 or '38
exiled from Germany banned & blazing black jacket —
that everything
in a time of all things in collapse
that embrace that particular set of syllables of a sudden attack
or just a breath of a song
the one I would hear back in the early '50's
when I walked the barren earth with my mother & father
the sound
of One when Luz still lived & Felipe still parted the red lands
& no one knew we existed in the fires
the flames that consume all of us
now

Ten Thousand Lives

i
was
going

to tell you about Victor Martinez and his love of Nabokov
in that tiny room we used to sublet on 24th & Capp Street #10
second floor across the street where Cecilia designed *Akrílica*
in '88 — about
his love for Heidegger & Nietzsche & the Chinese classics
what I mean
is his insistence on deciphering the way of things not
the pettiness of our lives
of our political & cultural entanglement with you he wanted
      to pierce the Quantum
                 of it all of us all
                           where imagination duplicates

into all being in mitosis & in doing so
thinking & mind — he is gone
now in that
room where we talked & thought & invented our liberations &
   were
       reborn

Address Book for the Firefly

on the Road North #6

here a river — you can stop
you can bathe & rest

you can meditate on
water & stones & the flow

you can note
the breath sound
of all our lives

come with me

come with me:

I will be writing —

ven conmigo:

escribiré —

with one letter the story of our lives
we will be dancing strangers under the honeyed yellow light
we will bathe deep together

con una letra historia de nuestras vidas
seremos dos extraños bailando
bajo la luz de amarillo meloso
nos bañaremos profundamente juntos

the cinnamon-scented candle flames will be weaving
they will be revealing to us their secret designs
we will touch our faces slowly   slowly

las llamas de las velas con aroma a canela entretejiéndose
nos revelarán sus diseños secretos
nos tocaremos los rostros lentamente   lentamente

for a moment after we play
after we unfold and lay upon the carpets after the waters
wash away our wounds and scald our scars
    we will speak of our mothers and fathers who

por un momento después de jugar
después de desplegarnos tendidos sobre la alfombra
después de que las aguas
hayan lavado nuestras heridas y escaldado nuestras cicatrices
    hablaremos de nuestras madres y nuestros padres quienes

journeyed all their lives on wagons on foot and trains
    leaning toward the fickle moon of paradise
    who dreamed us as they rushed further from us
        we will meditate on our mothers' names

viajaron toda la vida en vagones a pie en trenes
    inclinándose hacia la voluble luna del paraíso
    quienes nos soñaron a medida que se apresuraban lejos de
nosotros
        meditaremos en los nombres de nuestras madres

Lucía

        Aramara

            María

    Dolores —

in lost languages we will whisper
their unwritten wishes —

en lenguas ya perdidas susurraremos
sus anhelos no escritos —

Montaña

                              Piedra

Incienso

Mar

we will speak of their scarves and hats
their sandals and pilgrimage satchels the wild reddish fruit
they peeled and opened to give us life

hablaremos de sus bufandas y sus sombreros
de sus sandalias y sus bolsas de peregrinación la fruta roja y
    salvaje
que pelaron y abrieron para darnos vida

our hands will join and then lift as we
step to the fires at the center of this umber clay floor
sewn with leaves stones and branches and reeds
we will notice the unwinding flames their unending quest
toward something we do not know

nuestras manos se unirán y luego se alzarán a medida que
nos acercamos a las hogueras en el centro de este oscuro piso
    de barro
bordado con hojas piedras y ramas y juncos
notaremos sus llamas que se desenrollan su dicha infinita
hacia algo que no conocemos

             we will sing again
we will twirl again
we will be renewed again with each other's breath
graze graze   each other's shoulders we will

             cantaremos de nuevo
giraremos de nuevo
nos renovaremos de nuevo con el aliento de uno y otro
rozar rozar   mutuamente nuestros hombros nos

we will kneel as if the last   facing each other
pouring sweetened milk into earthen bowls
carved with the signs of those things that
burn across the blackish light every 2,000 years

arrodillaremos como los últimos   uno frente al otro
vertiendo leche endulzada en cuencos de arcilla
labrados con los signos de aquellas cosas que
arden a través de la luz negruzca cada 2,000 años

this is when we will almost smile as children almost smile
in the flecked dawn before they   move the forms of noon-light

es entonces cuando casi sonreiremos como los niños casi sonríen
en la moteada aurora antes de   mover las formas de luz del
     mediodía

we will be close to happiness the goal of our lives
I will call your name for the first time

Warrior
                    River's infinite eye
          Caller of creation

you will say mine
you will say

estaremos cerca de la felicidad la meta de nuestras vidas
llamaré tu nombre por vez primera

Guerrera
                    Ojo infinito del río
          Llamadora de la creación

tú pronunciarás el mío
tú dirás

Water

you will say

Wind leaf horse

Agua

tú dirás

Caballo hoja viento

again we will dance long
circling each other with our beads flashing
embracing all our lovers and enemies
with our meditations bequeathed from our grandmothers

de nuevo bailaremos largamente
haciendo círculos uno en torno al otro con nuestras cuentas
    brillando
abrazando a todos nuestros amantes y enemigos
con las meditaciones que nos legaron nuestras abuelas

Angustia

sangre

        bravura   *mesa*

we will sit for a minute or two for a day or two
and sweat in silence

nos sentaremos un minuto o dos por un día o dos
y sudaremos en silencio

we will chant our many births
about the abyss and the aurora
about the sacred dizziness   as we broke
    through all the cries of wars and redemptions of being
                    — this blurred world

cantaremos nuestros múltiples nacimientos
al filo del abismo y de la aurora
al filo del sagrado mareo a medida que irrumpimos
    entre todos los gritos de guerra y redenciones de ser
                    — este mundo borroso

we will greet each other once again
I will write in rhythms as the words come to me
you will walk in — this is my hope

nos saludaremos de nuevo
yo escribiré en ritmos así como las palabras vienen a mí
tú entrarás — esta es mi esperanza

Translation to Spanish by Lauro Flores

"We must develop a sense of oneness of 7 billion human beings"
— *Dalai Lama*